Orton Gillingham Decodable Readers

Easy decodable texts to improve reading and writing skills
in struggling readers and kids with dyslexia

Volume 2

Rebecca T. Wilkerson

Introduction

Teaching a child with dyslexia to read: Dyslexia is a specific and persistent learning disability that affects reading and writing. For children with dyslexia, learning to read and write can be a difficult challenge for families and educators to tackle. For these children, written language becomes a great barrier, often without meaning or logic, which generates rejection of the task, frustration and discomfort.

The child with dyslexia is a child who has significant difficulties in reading and writing, because their brain processes information differently than other children; which is why if we expect the same results following the traditional method, we will find many barriers that can and often do harm the child. It is important to become aware of the characteristics of this difficulty, so as to help the child learn to read and the consequent overcoming of their difficulties such as understanding, knowledge and attention to their needs.

Reading difficulties with dyslexia

Dyslexia is a learning disability of neurobiological origin, which causes seem to be in the maturation and structuring of certain brain structures.

Dyslexia is therefore a condition of the brain which causes it to process information differently, making it difficult for the person to understand letters, their sounds, their combinations, etc.

Human language is a language based on signs, letters and their sounds, which are arbitrary. The correspondence of each grapheme (letter) with its phoneme (sound), does not follow any logic; it's simply chance. This is one of the greatest difficulties that children face when they have to learn to read and write. Converting the spoken language, the know into signs and transforming sounds into letters is a challenge.

This is even more complicated in children with dyslexia; the relationship becomes something indecipherable for them. No matter how hard they try, they cannot make sense of that dance between letters and sounds.

Children with dyslexia have a lot of difficulty recognizing letters; sometimes they mistake letters for others, write them backwards, etc.

Another difficulty they face, is knowing the sound that corresponds to each letter; and things get even more complicated when we combine several letters and we have to know several sounds.

New words are a challenge for them and they can forget them easily, so they must work hard to acquire them. Sometimes they read certain words effortlessly, but the next day they completely forget them.

When they write, they omit letters, change their position, forget words in a sentence, etc.

Dyslexia also affects reading comprehension. When they read they are trying really hard to decipher and understand each word, sometimes even each letter; that is why the meaning of the text gets lost.

Reading comprehension: Activities to help develop it in children

How to teach a child with dyslexia to read

A child with dyslexia has difficulty learning to read and write, because it is hard for them to recognize letters and know which sound they correspond to. However, the child can learn to read and write and overcome those difficulties. Remember that dyslexia is a learning difficulty that does not imply any physical or mental handicap; the child with dyslexia has adequate capacities. In order to teach a child with dyslexia to read, it is essential to know the nature of their difficulties, understand them and use a teaching method that responds to their needs.

A child with dyslexia

A teaching method to help a child with dyslexia read.

In the first place, it is necessary to make an assessment of the child, to know their reading and writing level, the nature and characteristics of their difficulties in order to understand their specific needs. For this, it is advisable to seek a specialist.

Reading favors the development of phonological awareness (which consists of the correspondence of the sound with the letter). To do this, start with simple activities, letter by letter. Even if other children around the same age read full texts, it may be necessary to start working letter by letter. Later, we can continue with the words, phrases and texts. It is about dedicating more time and more detail to the learning process.

Phonological awareness worksheets

Use motivational activities that are engaging. Do not limit the child to just paper and pencil: they can make letters out of play dough, write on sand with their fingers, play catch or games such as hangman, word searches, crossword puzzles, etc.
Don't force them to read or read a lot. Try to have them read on a daily basis, little by little; sometimes a sentence or a paragraph is enough. Help them understand what they read, ask them questions, ask them to read again, etc.

TABLE OF CONTENTS

Final Blend 'ck'............................page 1-14

Final Blend 'nk'...........................page 15-30

Final Blend 'sk'...........................page 31-44

Final Blend 'rk'...........................page 45-59

Final Blend 'nd'...........................page 60-73

Final Blend 'rd'...........................page 74-87

Find the words........................page 88-89

Resources..............................Page 90-112

Read the story. Identify and underline all the 'ck' words.

'ck'

Lucky Bucky

Bucky is the name of a yellow duck. Bucky has a long neck. Bucky is a lucky duck. Whenever bucky pecks his beak in the water it catches a fish. All the ducks call him "lucky Bucky". Bucky has a friend named Puck. Puck is a white duck. Puck and Bucky spend their day sitting on their favorite rock at the dock. They peck, lick and quack all day long. Bucky likes to sit in the muck. "Yuck Yuck!" says Puck. "Don't sit there." Bucky is quick. He comes out of the muck.

Write all the 'ck' words that you have found in the story.				

Read the story and fill in the blank spaces with the appropriate words.

Lucky Bucky

ck

- Bucky is the name of a yellow _____.
- Bucky has a long _____.
- Bucky is a lucky _____.
- Whenever _____ pecks his beak in the water it catches a fish.
- All the ducks call him "_____ Bucky".
- Bucky has a friend named _____.
- _____ is a white duck. Puck and Bucky spend their day sitting on their favorite _____ at the dock.
- They _____, lick and _____ all day long.
- Bucky likes to sit in the _____.
- "_____ _____!" says Puck.

Write any ten 'ck' words.				

Read the story and circle whether the statement is true or false. If the statement is false, provide the correct answer for it.

ck

Bucky is the name of a white duck.

True   False

_____
_____

Bucky has a long beak.

True   False

_____
_____

Puck is a lucky duck.

True   False

_____
_____

Puck and Sandy spend their day sitting on their favorite rock at the dock.

True   False

_____
_____
_____

Bucky likes to sit in the muck.

_____
_____

Read the story 'Lucky Bucky' and answer the following questions.

Who is the lucky duck?

_____

_____

_____

_____

Why do all the ducks call Bucky, "Lucky Bucky"?

_____

_____

_____

_____

Who is Bucky's best friend?

_____

_____

_____

_____

How do Puck and Bucky spend their day?

_____

_____

_____

_____

Bucky is the name of a yellow duck. | 8

Bucky has a long neck. | 13

Bucky is a lucky duck. | 18

Whenever bucky pecks his beak in | 30

the water it catches a fish. | 37

All the ducks call him "lucky Bucky". | 43

Bucky has a friend named Puck. | 48

Puck is a white duck. | 62

Puck and Bucky spend their day sitting

on their favorite rock at the dock.

They peck, lick and quack all day long. | 70

Bucky likes to sit in the muck. | 77

"Yuck Yuck!" says Puck. | 81

"Don't sit there." | 84

Bucky is quick. | 87

He comes out of the muck. | 93

Date			
Words per minute			
Number of Errors			

Read the story. Identify and underline all the 'ck' words.

ck

Words to read and highlight			
Nickie	Jack	pack	picked
checked	black	neck	locked

Jack and Nickie

Nickie is packing for her trip. Jack asked Nickie, "What should I pack for the trip?". Nickie said, "Don't forget to pack your socks and favorite clock." Nickie picked all her beautiful frocks with matching necklaces and packed them in the suitcase. Nickie locked the suitcase after checking all her things. "When will we be back from the trip?" asked Jack. Nickie said, "We will be back in a week, don't forget to pack your black shoes and red jacket." Nickie forgot to pack her neck pillow. Jack saw the neck pillow lying beside the checkerboard. Jack gave the neck pillow to his sister.

Write all the 'ck' words that you have found in the story.

Read the story "Jack and Nickie" and fill in the blank spaces with the appropriate words.

ck

Point and say the sounds.				
sh	k	x	p	ng
t	ch	p	ck	q

Jack and Nickie

Nickie is _____ for her trip. _____ asked Nickie, "What should I _____ for the trip?". Nickie said, "Don't forget to _____ your _____ and favorite clock." Nickie picked all her beautiful _____ with matching _____ and packed them in the suitcase. Nickie _____ the suitcase after checking all her things. "When we will be _____ from the trip?" asked _____. Nickie said, "We will be back in a week, don't forget to pack your _____ shoes and red _____." Nickie forgot to pack her _____ pillow. Jack saw the neck pillow lying beside the _____. Jack gave the neck pillow to his sister.

The teacher will dictate some words and the students will write them below.

_____	_____	_____
_____	_____	_____

Read the story "Jack and Nickie" and answer the following questions.

Who is packing for the trip?

_____

_____

_____

How long will the trip last?

_____

_____

_____

What did Nickie keep in the suitcase?

_____

_____

_____

What did Jack pack for the trip?

_____

_____

_____

Write rhyming words for the
words written below.

ck

rock			
sock			
pack			
check			
stick			
peck			
rack			
prick			
back			

Assess the fluency by writing the number of words read, per minute.

Nickie is packing for her trip.	6
Jack asked Nickie, "What should I pack for the trip?"	16
Nickie said, "Don't forget to pack your socks and favorite clock."	27
Nickie picked all her beautiful frocks with matching necklaces and packed them in the suitcase.	42
Nickie locked the suitcase after checking all her things.	51
"When will we be back from the trip?" asked Jack.	61
Nickie said, "We will be back in a week, don't forget to pack your black shoes and red jacket."	80
Nickie forgot to pack her neck pillow.	87
Jack saw the neck pillow lying beside the checkerboard.	96
Jack gave the neck pillow to his sister.	104

Date			
Words per minute			
Number of Errors			

ck

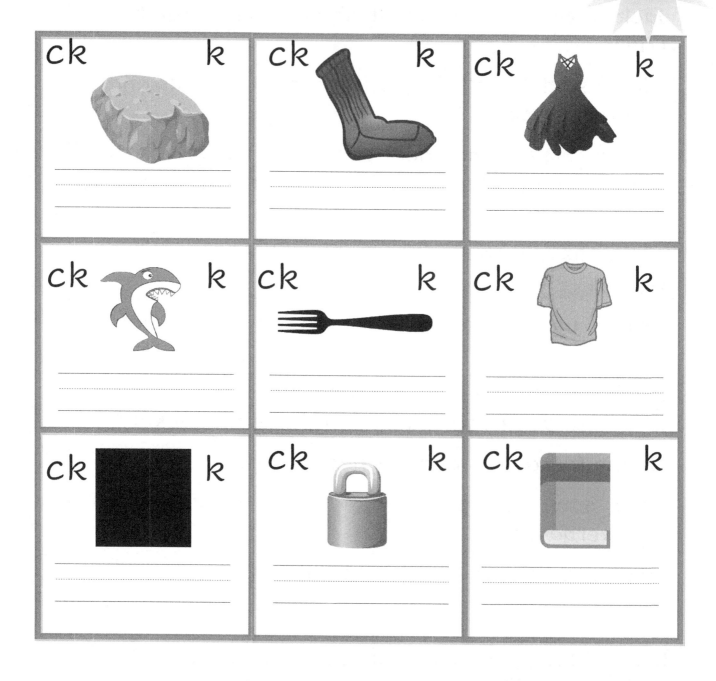

ck k	ck k	ck k
ck k	ck k	ck k
ck k	ck k	ck k

11

Make sentences using the words written below.

ck

Rock

Sack

Lock

Rack

Pack

Dock

Knock

Lack

Deck

Wreck

Sack

A B C D E F G H I J K L M N O P

Find and circle the words written below.

ck

Sock	lock	dock	rock
Lack	pack	deck	knock

s	h	k	n	o	c	k	p
h	o	d	e	c	k	k	l
a	g	c	w	h	i	p	a
l	h	e	k	t	v	m	c
o	w	h	y	a	n	s	k
c	p	a	c	k	v	i	e
k	f	j	d	o	c	k	l
e	r	o	c	k	m	w	k

1

Write a story using any five words from the word bank.

ck

Rock brick trick prick tick
Jack whack stock stick
back check lock truck pack

Read the story. Identify and underline all the 'nk' words.

nk

The Pink trunk

Mom told Josh to clean the junk from his room. She asked him to put all his old toys in the pink trunk. Mom said, "Think wisely and choose all the toys that can be given to charity." Josh was blank for a while. He drank milk and started to think. Josh dunked a chunk of cookie into the milk and ate it. In a blink of an eye, he made up his mind. Josh saw a box under the bunk bed. He found a toy monk and a funny skunk to put inside the pink tank. He also put a piggy bank, an ink pen, soldier's tank and a beautiful plank in the pink trunk.

Write all the 'nk' words that you have found in the story.				

Read the story and fill in the blank
spaces with the appropriate words.

nk

junk	blank	think	
drank	dunk	bunk	
pink	blink	bank	tank
chunk	monk	skunk	ink

The Pink Trunk

Mom told Josh to clean the _____ from his room.

She asked him to put all his old toys in the _____ trunk.

Mom said, "_____ wisely and choose all the toys that can be given to charity."

Josh was _____ for a while.

He _____ milk and started to _____.

Josh _____ed a _____ of cookie into the milk and ate it.

In a _____ of an eye, he made up his mind.

Josh saw a box under the _____ bed.

He found a toy _____ and a funny _____ to put inside the pink tank.

He also put a piggy _____, an _____ pen, soldier's _____ and a beautiful plank in the _____ trunk.

Read the story and circle whether the statement is true or false. If the statement is false, provide the correct answer for it.

nk

Mom told Josh to clean the toys from his room.

True   False

_____
_____
_____
_____

Mom said, "Think wisely and choose all the toys that can be given to charity."

True   False

_____
_____
_____
_____

He drank juice and started to think. Josh saw a toy under the bunk bed.

True   False

_____
_____
_____
_____

He also put a piggy bank, an ink pen, soldier's tank and a beautiful blanket in the pink trunk.

True   False

_____
_____
_____
_____

Read the story 'The Pink Trunk' and answer the following questions.

What did mom say to Josh?

_____
_____
_____
_____

Where was the box kept?

_____
_____
_____
_____

Write the names of the objects josh found and kept in the pink trunk.

_____
_____
_____
_____
_____
_____
_____

'nk'

Mom told Josh to clean the junk from his room. | 10

She asked him to put all his old toys in the pink trunk. | 23

Mom said, "Think wisely and chose all those toys which can be given to the charity." | 39

Josh was blank for a while. | 45

He drank milk and started to think. | 52

Josh dunked a chunk of cookie into the milk and ate it. | 64

Within a blink of an eye, he made his mind. | 74

Josh saw a box under the bunk bed. | 82

He found a toy monk and a funny skunk to put inside the pink tank. | 97

He also put a piggy bank, an ink pen, soldier's tank and a beautiful plank in the pink trunk. | 116

Date			
Words per minute			
Number of Errors			

Write the name of each picture and listen to the ending sound. Circle 'nk' or 'k'.

nk

nk k	nk k	nk k
_____	_____	_____
nk k	nk k	nk k
_____	_____	_____
nk k	nk k	nk k
_____	_____	_____

Make sentences using the words written below.

nk

Tank

Trunk

Bunk

Think

Drink

Pink

Skunk

Dunk

Bank

Plank

Ink

Find and circle the words written below.

nk

Skunk   punk   dunk   ink

Think   bank   trunk   bunk

b	h	t	r	u	n	k	b
u	o	f	k	c	k	k	a
n	d	u	n	k	i	p	n
k	h	e	k	t	v	m	k
o	w	n	y	a	n	s	k
c	t	h	i	n	k	i	i
k	f	j	p	u	n	k	n
s	k	u	n	k	m	w	k

> **Read the story. Identify and underline all the 'nk' words.**
>
> **nk**

Frank goes to the Bank

Frank needed to go to the bank. He ironed the wrinkle shirt and wore it. He checked his car's tank. The tank was filled up with gas. On the way to the bank, Frank saw an old man sitting on a wooden plank. Frank drove by the junkyard and saw a pink vintage car. Frank went blank while watching the pink car. Cars started honking behind Frank's car. "Honk, honk! Start driving man!" Said the man, driving beside Frank's car. Franked winked at the man and said, I am sorry man!" Frank stopped thinking about the pink vintage car and started driving again. Frank saw a punk walking on the road. Frank stopped the car at the traffic signal and saw a monkey siting on the tree trunk. The monkey was eating a chunk of bread and drinking juice. Frank reached the bank and parked the car.

Write all the 'nk' words that you have found in the story.				

Read the story and fill in the blank spaces with the appropriate words.

nk

wrinkle	Frank	junk
blank	honk	think
punk	wink	pink
plank	tank	bank
Monkey	drink	chunk

Frank needed to go to the _____. He ironed the _____ shirt and wore it. He checked his car's _____. The tank was filled up with gas. On the way to the bank _____ saw an old man sitting on a wooden _____. Frank drove by the _____yard and saw a _____ vintage car. Frank went _____ while watching the _____ car. Cars started _____ing behind Frank's car. "Honk, _____! Start driving man!" Said the man, driving beside _____'s car. Frank _____ed at the man and said, I am sorry man!" Frank stopped _____ing about the _____ vintage car and started driving again. Frank saw a _____ walking on the road. Frank stopped the car at the traffic signal and saw a _____ siting on the tree trunk. The _____ was eating a _____ of bread and _____ juice. Frank reached the bank and parked the car.

> **Read the story and circle whether the statement is true or false. If the statement is false, provide the correct answer for it.**

Frank needed to go to the bank.

       True   False

_____
_____

The car's tank had no gas.

       True   False

_____
_____

Frank saw an old man sitting on a wooden bench.

       True   False

_____
_____
_____
_____

Franked smiled at the man and said, I am sorry man!"

       True   False

_____
_____
_____
_____

Frank saw a punk walking on the road.

       True   False

_____
_____
_____

Read the story 'Frank goes to the Bank' and answer the following questions.

1. Where was Frank going?

2. Frank's mind was occupied thinking about something. Can you describe what he was thinking about?

3. Where did Frank see a monkey?

4. What was the monkey doing?

Assess the fluency by writing the number of words read per minute.

Frank needed to go to the bank.	7
He ironed the wrinkle shirt and wore it.	15
He checked his car's tank.	20
The tank was filled up with gas.	27
On the way to the bank, Frank saw an old man sitting on a wooden plank.	43
Frank drove by the junkyard and saw a pink vintage car.	54
Frank went blank while watching the pink car.	62
Cars started honking behind Frank's car.	68
"Honk, honk! Start driving man!"	73
Said the man, driving beside Frank's car.	80
Franked winked at the man and said, I am sorry man!"	91
Frank stopped thinking about the pink vintage car and started driving again.	103
Frank saw a punk walking on the road.	111
Frank stopped the car at the traffic signal and saw a monkey siting on the tree trunk.	128
The monkey was eating a chunk of bread and drinking juice.	139
Frank reached the bank and parked the car.	147

Date			
Words per minute			
Number of Errors			

Write rhyming words for the words written below.

nk

monk			
bank			
monkey			
donkey			
sink			
wink			
bunk			
trunk			
tank			

28

Make sentences using the words written below.

nk

Rack

Bank

Tank

Think

Blink

Sink

Bunk

Monk

dunk

Drink

Link

Write a story using any five words from the word bank.

nk

Link	mink	sink	rink
think	tank	rank	bank
chipmunk	drink	plank	prank

Read the story. Identify and underline all the 'sk' words.

sk

Words to read and highlight				
dusk	husk	tusk	mask	brisk
disk	whisk	task	flask	desk

Mask's Task

The teacher gave Jim a task. Jim asked the teacher, "What is the task, Miss? The teacher told Jim, "You have to make an animal mask by dusk tomorrow." Jim walked briskly and went home. Jim took out a box with junk, maybe he could find something he could use for the mask. He found an empty flask, a whisk, a tusk, a disk and some husk. Jim sat down on the desk and started working on the mask. He looked at all the objects he found from the junk box and thought to make an elephant mask using the tusk, disk and husk.

Write all the 'sk' words that you have found in the story.

Read the story "Mask's Task" and fill in the blank spaces with the appropriate words.

sk

Point and say the sounds.				
sk	st	nt	nk	pt
sp	sk	nd	ct	mp

Mask's Task

The teacher gave Jim a _____. Jim asked the teacher, "What is the _____, Miss? The teacher told Jim, "You have to make an animal _____ by _____ tomorrow." Jim walked _____ly and went home. Jim took out a box with _____, maybe he could find something he could use for the _____. He found an empty _____, a _____, a _____, a _____ and some _____. Jim sat down on the _____ and started working on the _____. He looked at all the objects he _____ from the junk box and thought to make an elephant mask using the tusk, disk and _____.

The teacher will dictate some words and the students will write them below.

Read the story and circle whether the statement is true or false. If the statement is false, provide the correct answer for it.

The teacher asked Jim to make a poster.

True   False

_____
_____

Jim decided to make an animal poster.

True   False

_____
_____

Jim found an empty box, a whisk, a brush, a pen and some husk.

True   False

_____
_____
_____
_____

Jim sat down on the desk and started working on the mask.

True   False

_____
_____
_____
_____

He looked at all the objects he found from the junk box and thought to make a poster.

True   False

_____
_____
_____
_____

Read the story "Mask's Task" and answer the following questions.

Who gave Jim a task to do?

_____

_____

What was the task?

_____

_____

_____

_____

Write the names of the objects Jim found from the junk.

_____

_____

_____

_____

Write the names of the objects Jim decided to use to make the mask.

_____

_____

_____

Assess the fluency by writing the number of words read per minute.

'sk'

The teacher gave Jim a task.	6
Jim asked the teacher, "What is the task, Miss?	15
The teacher told Jim, "You have to make an animal mask by dusk tomorrow."	29
Jim walked briskly and went home.	35
Jim took out a box with junk, maybe he could find something he could use for the mask.	53
He found an empty flask, a whisk, a tusk, a disk and some husk.	67
Jim sat down on the desk and started working on the mask.	79
He looked at all the objects he found from the junk box and thought to make an elephant mask using the tusk, disk and husk.	104

Date			
Words per minute			
Number of Errors			

Read the story. Identify and underline all the 'sk' words.

sk

Corn's Husk

Sasha was sitting on the desk, working on her final task. She was drawing an elephant's tusk. She was feeling hungry and was waiting for the bell to ring so that she could eat, but first she would have to remove the corn's husk. But the period was not over yet. The teacher said, "You can ask me if you have any questions. The notes are kept on the desk." Sasha looked at the watch and the bell rang. Sasha jumped up and whisked out of the classroom. Sasha was so hungry that she risked jumping over the fence which was not allowed. Sasha tripped over on a cat which was basking in the sun. She yelled, "Please help!"

Write all the 'sk' words that you have found in the story.

Read the story "Corn's Husk" and fill in the blank spaces with the appropriate words.

sk

Point and say the sounds.				
sp	mp	ct	rp	rt
nt	sk	rm	rn	mb

Sasha was sitting on the _____, working on her final _____. She was drawing an elephant's _____. She was feeling hungry and was waiting for the bell to ring so that she could eat, but first she would have to remove the corn's husk. But the period was not over yet. The teacher said, "You can _____ me if you have any questions. The notes are kept on the _____." Sasha looked at the watch and the bell rang. Sasha jumped up and _____ed out of the classroom. Sasha was so hungry that she _____ed jumping over the fence which was not allowed. Sasha tripped over on a cat which was _____ing in the sun. She yelled, "Please help!"

The teacher will dictate some words and the students will write them below.

Read the story and circle whether the statement is true or false. If the statement is false, provide the correct answer for it.

Sasha was sitting on the chair, working on her final task.

True   False

_____

_____

She was feeling hungry and was waiting for the bell to ring so that she could eat pancakes.

True   False

_____

_____

_____

_____

The teacher said, "You can ask me if you have any questions. The notes are kept on the shelf."

True   False

_____

_____

_____

_____

Sasha jumped up and whisked out of the classroom.

True   False

_____

_____

Her teacher came over and helped her.

True   False

_____

_____

Read the story "Corn's husk" and answer the following questions.

Where was Sasha sitting?

_____
_____
_____
_____

What was Sasha waiting for?

_____
_____
_____
_____

What was Sasha's final task?

_____
_____
_____
_____

How did Sasha get hurt?

_____
_____
_____
_____

Assess the fluency by writing the number of words read per minute.

'sk'

Sasha was sitting on the desk, working on her final task.	11
She was drawing an elephant's tusk.	17
She was feeling hungry and was waiting for the bell to ring so that she could eat, but first she would have to remove the corn's husk.	44
But the period was not over yet.	51
The teacher said, "You can ask me if you have any questions.	63
The notes are kept on the desk."	70
Sasha looked at the watch and the bell rang.	79
Sasha jumped up and whisked out of the classroom.	88
Sasha was so hungry that she risked jumping over the fence which was not allowed.	103
Sasha tripped over on a cat which was basking in the sun.	115
She yelled, "Please help!"	119
Her friend came over and helped her.	126

Date			
Words per minute			
Number of Errors			

40

Write rhyming words for the
words written below.

sk

husk			
ask			
task			
bask			
desk			
whisk			
brisk			
tusk			
risk			

Write the name of each picture and listen to the ending sound. Circle 'sk' or 'ck'.

sk

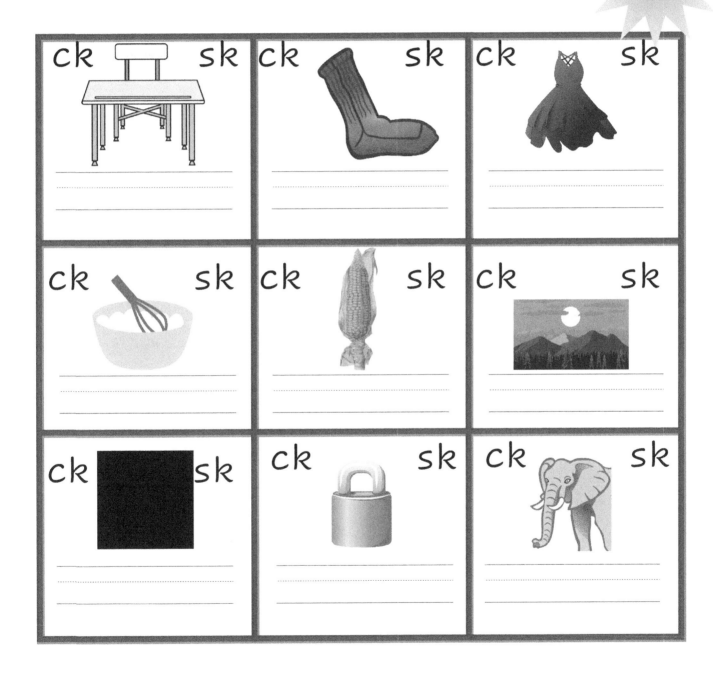

ck   sk

ck   sk

ck   sk

ck   sk

ck   sk

ck   sk

ck   sk

ck   sk

ck   sk

Make sentences using the words written below.

sk

Husk

Dusk

Tusk

Risk

Brisk

Desk

Ask

Whisk

Mask

Desk

Task

43

Write a story using any five words from the word bank.

sk

Ask   mask   task   risk

whisk   husk   disk   desk

frisk   musk   unmask

Clark the Clerk

Clark works as a clerk at an office. He eats his lunch with his special silver fork. He likes to eat pork. Clark the clerk removes the bottle cork and looks everywhere for a glass. He looks for a glass in the kitchen. The kitchen is dark. Clark turns the light on and finds a glass to pour his drink. Clark smirks and finishes his lunch. Clark goes to the park for a walk. A dog barks at Clark. Clark feeds him the leftover pork. Clark bumps into a stork. "What a dork I am!" Says Clark. "I am sorry, I will mark your spot! Stork." Says, Clark to the Stork.

Write all the 'rk' words that you have found in the story.				

rk

Clark the Clerk

Clark works as a _____ at an office. He eats his lunch with his special silver _____. He likes to eat _____. Clark the clerk removes the bottle _____ and looks everywhere for a glass. He looks for a glass in the kitchen. The kitchen is _____. Clark turns the light on and finds a glass to pour his _____. Clark _____ and finishes his lunch. Clark goes to the _____ for a walk. A dog _____ at Clark. Clark feeds him the leftover _____. Clark bumps into a _____. "What a _____, I am!" Says Clark. "I am sorry, I will _____ your spot! _____." Says, _____ to the Stork.

Write any ten words ending with 'rk'.				

46

Read the story and circle whether the statement is true or false. If the statement is false, provide the correct answer for it.

Clark works at an office as an officer.

True   False

_____
....
_____

He eats his lunch with his special silver spoon.

True   False

_____
....
_____

He likes to eat chicken.

True   False

_____
....
_____

Clark the clerk removes the bottle cap and looks everywhere for a glass.

True   False

_____
....
_____
....
_____

Clark goes to the park for a walk.

True   False

_____
....
_____

Read the story "Clark the Clerk" and answer the following questions.

Where does Clark work? Write his job position.

How does Clark eat his lunch?

What happened when Clark could not find a glass?

Why was the dog barking at Clark?

Clark works as a clerk at an office.	8
He eats his lunch with his special silver fork.	17
He likes to eat pork.	22
Clark the clerk removes the bottle cork and looks everywhere for a glass.	35
He looks for a glass in the kitchen.	43
The kitchen is dark.	47
Clark turns the light on and finds a glass to pour his drink.	60
Clark smirks and finishes his lunch.	68
Clark goes to the park for a walk.	74
A dog barks at Clark.	79
Clark feeds him the leftover pork.	85
Clark bumps into a stork.	90
"What a dork I am!" Says Clark.	97
"I am sorry, I will mark your spot! Stork."	106
Says, Clark to the Stork.	111

Date			
Words per minute			
Number of Errors			

Read the story. Identify and underline all the 'rk' words.

rk

Burk's Artwork

Burk lives in Denmark. Burk has a brown birthmark on his left cheek. He is in third grade. He believes in teamwork. Burk always completes his homework on time. Burk is always first in finishing his classwork. No one is as sharp as Burk. Burk's teacher calls him little artist because of his exceptional artwork. His artwork includes a beautiful shark made out of recycled papers and an ark made with toothpicks. Burk also made a park using different cardboard pieces. One of Burk's artworks was a view of a dark night. Burk won a prize at an art competition for making a stork out of cotton and feathers. All the students lurk at Burk's craftwork, whenever he is in the middle of an artwork.

Write all the 'rk' words that you have found in the story.

50

Read the story "Burk's Artwork" and fill in the blank spaces with the appropriate words.

rk

Point and say the sounds.				
sh	wh	rk	ck	nt
mp	ch	st	mb	ph

Burk lives in _____. Burk has a brown _____ on his left cheek. He is in third grade. He believes in _____. Burk always completes his _____ on time. Burk is always first in finishing his _____. No one is as sharp as Burk. Burk's teacher calls him little artist because of his exceptional _____. His artwork includes a beautiful _____ made out of recycled papers and an _____ made with toothpicks. Burk also made a _____ using different cardboard pieces. One of Burk's artworks was a view of a _____ night. Burk won a prize at an art competition for making a _____ out of cotton and feathers. All the students _____ at Burk's _____, whenever he is in the middle of an artwork.

The teacher will dictate some words and the students will write them below.

Read the story and circle whether the statement is true or false. If the statement is false, provide the correct answer for it.

Burk lives in Paris.

True   False

_____

Burk has a black birthmark on his left cheek.

True   False

_____

Burk always completes his homework on time.

True   False

_____

Burk's teacher calls him little artist because of his exceptional paintings.

True   False

_____

_____

Burk also made a park using different cloth pieces.

True   False

_____

**Read the story "Burk's Artwork" and
answer the following questions.**

Where does Burk live?

_____

_____

What kind of birthmark does Burk have?

_____

_____

_____

_____

Why does Burk's teacher call him little artist? Write
in detail about Burk's artworks.

_____

_____

_____

_____

_____

_____

_____

_____

_____

_____

Assess the fluency by writing the number of words read per minute. 'rk'

Burk lives in Denmark.	4
Burk has a brown birthmark on his left cheek.	13
He is in third grade.	18
He believes in teamwork.	22
Burk always completes his homework on time.	29
Burk is always first in finishing his classwork.	37
No one is as sharp as Burk.	44
Burk's teacher calls him little artist because of his exceptional artwork.	55
His artwork includes a beautiful shark made out of recycled papers and an ark made with toothpicks.	72
Burk also made a park using different cardboard pieces.	81
One of Burk's artworks was a view of dark night.	91
Burk won a prize at an art competition for making a stork out of cotton and feathers.	108
All the students lurk at Burk's craftwork, whenever he is in the middle of an artwork.	124

Date			
Words per minute			
Number of Errors			

Write rhyming words for the words written below.

work			
homework			
ark			
shark			
lurk			
stork			
park			
dark			
smirk			

Write the name of each picture and listen to the beginning sound. Circle 'rk' or 'nk'.

rk

rk	nk	rk	nk	rk	nk
rk	nk	rk	nk	rk	nk
rk	nk	rk	nk	rk	nk

Write the words from the word bank in their appropriate places.

rk

Word Bank

shark   bark   dark   work

artwork   stork   fork

ark   mark   cork   spark

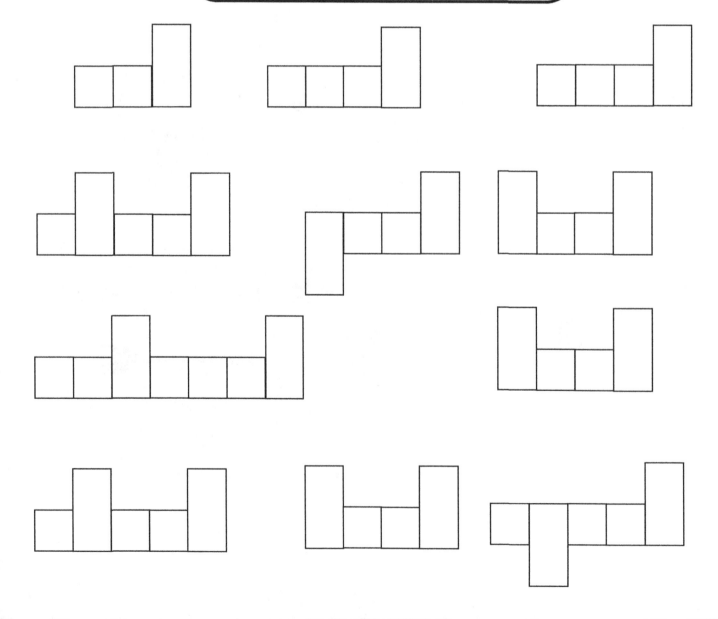

Find and circle the words written below.

rk

shark	ark	work
lurk	stork	pork
fork	dork	bark

k	h	l	u	r	k	s	p
r	s	w	r	h	j	k	k
o	g	h	w	o	r	k	r
p	h	e	a	t	v	m	o
b	w	h	y	r	n	s	f
a	s	t	o	r	k	i	e
r	f	j	x	h	b	r	l
k	l	d	o	r	k	w	a

Write a story using any five words from the word bank.

Work   smirk   dork   pork
lacework   bookmark   dark
bark   park   spark   shark

Read the story. Identify and underline all the 'nd' words.

nd

What's that sound in the pond?

Rand likes to sit beside the pond. Rand fantasizes about the nature that surrounds him. He has a round ball. Rand picks up the round ball from the ground. There is a beautiful pond in the sandy ground. Rand looks at all the small creatures in the pond. "Croak" "Croak", Rand hears a strange sound. "What's that sound in the pond?" The frog says, "It's me Rand. Croak, Croak. I'm making this sound. Can you help me send this message to my friend?" Rand says, "Let me help you send this message to your friend." "Quack" "Quack", Rand hears a strange sound coming from the pond. "What's that sound in the pond?" The duck says, "It's me Rand. Quack, Quack! I'm making this sound. Can you give me a hand? I want to come out of this pond." Rand says, "Let me give you a hand, to come out of the pond." "Buzz" "Buzz", Rand hears a strange sound. What's that sound in the pond? The bee says, "It's me Rand. "Buzz" "Buzz". I'm making this sound. Can you help me bend this flower stem? Rand says, "Let me help you bend this flower stem." Rand helped all the animals in the pond.

Write all the 'nd' words that you have found in the story.				

Read the story and fill in the blank spaces with the appropriate words.

nd

What's that sound in the pond?

Rand likes to sit beside the _____. Rand fantasizes about the nature that _____ him. He has a round ball. Rand picks up the _____ ball from the _____. There is a beautiful pond in the sandy ground. Rand looks at all the small creatures in the pond. "Croak" "Croak", Rand hears a strange _____. "What's that sound in the _____?" The frog says, "It's me Rand. Croak, Croak. I'm making this sound. Can you help me send this message to my _____?" Rand says, "Let me help you send this message to your friend." "Quack" "Quack", Rand hears a strange _____ coming from the pond. "What's that sound in the _____?" The duck says, "It's me Rand. Quack, Quack! I'm making this sound. Can you give me a _____? I want to come out of this pond." Rand says, "Let me give you a hand, to come out of the pond." "Buzz" "Buzz", Rand hears a strange sound. What's that sound in the pond? The bee says, "It's me Rand. "Buzz" "Buzz". I'm making this sound. Can you help me _____ this flower stem? Rand says, "Let me help you bend this flower stem." _____ helped all the animals in the pond.

Write any ten words ending with 'nd'.				

Read the story and circle whether the statement is true or false. If the statement is false, provide the correct answer for it.

nd

Rand likes to sit beside the pond.

True   False

_____

Rand picks up the round ball at the park.

True   False

_____

Donald looks at all the animals in the pond.

True   False

_____

"It's me Rand. Croak, Croak. I'm making this sound. Can you help me send this gift to my friend?"

True   False

_____

Rand helped all the frogs in the pond.

True   False

_____

Read the story "What's that sound in the pond?" and answer the following questions.

What does Rand like to do?

_____
....
_____
_____
....
_____

How many animals did Rand help at the pond?

_____
....
_____
_____
....
_____

Can you describe the different animal sounds that Rand heard at the pond?

_____
....
_____
_____
....
_____
_____
....
_____

7
15
20
29
38
55
67
69
73
83
95
106
118
130
138
152
159
171
173
177
185
195
203

Rand likes to sit beside the pond.

Rand fantasizes about the nature that surrounds him.

He has a round ball.

Rand picks up the round ball from the ground.

There is a beautiful pond in the sandy ground.

Rand looks at all the small creatures in the pond. "Croak" "Croak", Rand hears a strange sound.

"What's that sound in the pond?" The frog says, "It's me Rand.

Croak, Croak.

I'm making this sound.

Can you help me send this message to my friend?"

Rand says, "Let me help you send this message to your friend."

"Quack" "Quack", Rand hears a strange sound coming from the pond.

"What's that sound in the pond?" The duck says, "It's me Rand.

Quack, Quack! I'm making this sound. Can you give me a hand?

I want to come out of this pond."

Rand says, "Let me give you a hand, to come out of the pond."

"Buzz" "Buzz", Rand hears a strange sound.

What's that sound in the pond? The bee says, "It's me Rand.

"Buzz" "Buzz".

I'm making this sound.

Can you help me bend this flower stem?

Rand says, "Let me help you bend this flower stem."

Rand helped all the animals in the pond.

Date			
Words per minute			
Number of Errors			

Read the story. Identify and
underline all the 'nd' words.

'nd'

Sandy's Wand

Sandy is a kind girl. She has a magical wand. Sandy is really fond of her golden wand. Sandy goes to the beach. She wants to make the biggest sand castle ever. Sandy waves her wand in the air, wind starts blowing and a big sand castle appears in front of her. While playing in the big sand castle, a paper plane lands in front of Sandy. Sandy pretends to be the pilot of the plane and she plays with the paper plane. Sandy wants the plane to be grand. She looks all around the sand castle for her wand. But she could not find her wand. She sees a group of kids playing in a band. She goes up to the band and asks them, "Have you seen my brand-new golden magical wand?" The kids in the band reply, "We have not seen your brand-new wand. But we can help you find your magical wand". Sandy replies to them, "Thank you! It's very kind of you all."

Write all the 'nd' words that you have found in the story.

> **Read the story "Sandy's Wand" and fill in the blank spaces with the appropriate words.**

nd

Point and say the sounds.				
nt	wh	rd	ph	nd
nk	ch	st	ch	sh

Sandy is a _____ girl. She has a magical _____. Sandy is really fond of her golden wand. Sandy goes to the beach. She wants to make the biggest sand castle ever. Sandy waves her wand in the air, wind starts blowing and a big _____ castle appears in front of her. While playing in the big sand castle, a paper plane _____ in front of Sandy. Sandy pretends to be the pilot of the plane and she plays with the paper plane. Sandy wants the plane to be _____. She looks all around the sand castle for her wand. But she could not _____ her wand. She sees a group of kids playing in a _____. She goes up to the band and asks them, "Have you seen my _____-new golden magical wand?" The kids in the band reply, "We have not seen your brand-new _____. But we can help you find your magical wand". Sandy replies to them, "Thank you! It's very _____ of you all."

The teacher will dictate some words and the students will write them below.

Read the story "Sandy's Wand" and answer the following questions.

Who is Sandy?

_____
_____
_____

What is Sandy fond of?

_____
_____
_____

Where does Sandy go?

_____
_____
_____

How does a sand castle appear in front of Sandy?

_____
_____
_____
_____
_____
_____
_____

Where and how did Sandy lose her wand?

_____
_____
_____
_____

'nd'

Sandy is a kind girl.

She has a magical wand.

Sandy is really fond of her golden wand.

Sandy goes to the beach.

She wants to make the biggest sand castle ever.

Sandy waves her wand in the air, wind starts blowing and a big sand castle appears in front of her.

While playing in the big sand castle, a paper plane lands in front of Sandy.

Sandy pretends to be the pilot of the plane and she plays with the paper plane.

Sandy wants the plane to be grand.

She looks all around the sand castle for her wand.

But she could not find her wand.

She sees a group of kids playing in a band.

She goes up to the band and asks them, "Have you seen my brand-new golden magical wand?"

The kids in the band reply, "We have not seen your brand-new wand.

But we can help you find your magical wand".

Sandy replies to them, "Thank you! It's very kind of you all."

5
10
18
23
32
52
67
83
90
100
107
117
134
147
156
168

Date			
Words per minute			
Number of Errors			

Write rhyming words for the words written below.

nd

Pond			
wand			
friend			
pretend			
mend			
mind			
wind			
pond			

Write the name of each picture and listen to the ending sound. Circle 'nd' or 'd'.

nd

nd	d	nd	d	nd	d
nd	d	nd	d	nd	d
nd	d	nd	d	nd	d

Find and circle the words written below.

pond   friend   send

band   trend   brand

wand   bond   round

nd

b	o	n	d	e	o	h	p
h	s	e	n	d	j	b	h
f	r	i	e	n	d	r	r
w	h	o	p	s	v	a	d
a	w	h	u	h	n	n	n
n	h	w	c	n	a	d	e
d	d	p	o	n	d	i	r
o	b	a	n	d	e	w	t

Write the words from the word bank in their appropriate places.

nd

Word Bank

pond   brand   stand   and

hand   sand   end   grand

friend   weekend   strand

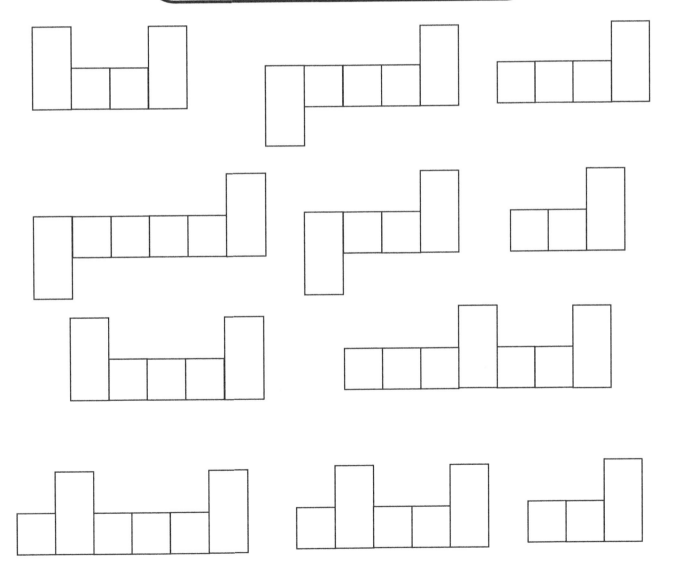

Write a story using any five
words from the word bank.

nd

And   mend   land   sand
hand   bend   attend   weekend
strand   friend   band   round

rd

The Nerd Bird

Once upon a time there lived a bird. His name was Richard. Everyone called him Nerd Richard. Richard the bird was a bookworm. He loved learning new words from the different stories he read. He read a wonderful story about a herd of sheep. The herd of sheep lived in a yard without any shepherd to take care of them. It was hard for the herd to protect themselves. A leopard roamed around the herd. All the sheep united and decided never to be alone. The herd went to the orchard fields and everywhere else as a group. The leopard never got the chance to attack the herd. Richard the bird learned the lesson on unity from the story.

Write all the 'rd' words that you have found in the story.				

rd

The Nerd Bird

Once upon a time there lived a _____. His name was _____. Everyone called him _____ Richard. Richard the bird was a bookworm. He loved learning new words from the different stories he read. He read a wonderful story about a _____ of sheep. The herd of sheep lived in a yard without any _____ to take care of them. It was _____ for the herd to protect themselves. A _____ roamed around the herd. All the sheep united and decided never to be alone. The herd went to the _____ fields and everywhere else as a group. The leopard never got the chance to attack the herd. Richard the bird learned the lesson on unity from the story.

Write any ten words ending with 'rd'.				

Read the story and circle whether the statement is true or false. If the statement is false, provide the correct answer for it.

Richard the owl was a bookworm.

True   False

_____

He loved learning new words from the different stories he read.

True   False

_____

The herd of sheep lived in a yard with a shepherd to take care of them.

True   False

_____

_____

A leopard roamed around the yard

True   False

_____

He read a wonderful story about a herd of sheep.

True   False

_____

Read the story "The Nerd Bird" and answer the following questions.

rd

Who was Richard?

_____
_____
_____

Why did everyone call Richard 'Nerd'?

_____
_____
_____

_____
_____

Write the story Richard read?

_____
_____
_____
_____

_____
_____
_____

_____
_____
_____

What was the moral of the story?

_____
_____
_____

Assess the fluency by writing the number of words read per minute.

rd

Once upon a time there lived a bird.	8
His name was Richard.	12
Everyone called him Nerd Richard.	17
Richard the bird was a bookworm.	23
He loved learning new words from the different stories he read.	34
He read a wonderful story about a herd of sheep.	44
The herd of sheep lived in a yard without any shepherd to take care of them.	60
It was hard for the herd to protect themselves.	69
A leopard roamed around the herd.	75
All the sheep united and decided never to be alone.	85
The herd went to the orchard fields and everywhere else as a group.	98
The leopard never got the chance to attack the herd.	108
Richard the bird learned the lesson on unity from the story.	119

Date			
Words per minute			
Number of Errors			

Read the story. Identify and underline all the 'rd' words.

rd

Royal Guard Archard

Archard is a security guard at the castle. He is a handsome man with a beard. He carries a sword with him. He marches attentively forward and backwards. He salutes and bows down when the king and queen are around. Archard accompanies the lord and his lady on their national tours. Archard accompanied the lord on his visits to the dockyard, vineyards and farmyards. Archard was rewarded with an award of bravery and loyalty. Archard wrote a thank you card to the royal family for their trust and care. Archard has one weird weakness, he is scared of lizards. Archard tries to overcome this awkward fear of lizards. He cannot afford to lose his position over this absurd fear.

Write all the 'rd' words that you have found in the story.

Read the story "Royal Guard Archard" and fill in the blank spaces with the appropriate words.

rd

Point and say the sounds.				
sh	wr	nk	ck	nt
m	ch	mp	b	ph

Archard is a security guard at the castle. He is a handsome man with a _____. He carries a _____ with him. He marches attentively _____ and _____. He salutes and bows down when the king and queen are _____. Archard accompanies the lord and his lady on their national tours. Archard accompanied the _____ on his visits to the _____, _____ and _____. Archard was rewarded with an award of bravery and loyalty. Archard wrote a thank you _____ to the royal family for their trust and care. Archard has one _____ weakness, he is scared of _____. Archard tries to overcome this _____ fear of _____. He cannot afford to lose his position over this _____ fear.

The teacher will dictate some words and the students will write them below.

Read the story "Royal Guard Archard" and answer the following questions.

Who is Archard?

_____
_____
_____

What does Archard do?

_____
_____
_____
_____
_____

What is Archard afraid of?

_____
_____
_____

What kind of reward was Archard awarded with?

_____
_____
_____
_____
_____

What does Archard do when the king and queen appear?

_____
_____
_____

Write rhyming words for the
words written below.

rd

word			
lord			
bird			
nerd			
curd			
ward			
board			
yard			
lizard			

Read the story 'Royal Guard Archard" and circle the wrong word in each sentence. Rewrite each sentence using the correct word.

rd

Archard is a security guard at the bank.

He carries a knife with him.

Archard was rewarded with an award of wisdom.

He is scared of snakes.

Richard tries to overcome this awkward fear of lizards.

Archard accompanies the king and his queen on their national tours.

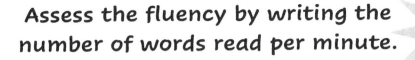

Assess the fluency by writing the number of words read per minute.

rd

8
16
22
28
40
51
64
74
89
99
108
119

Archard is a security guard at the castle.

He is a handsome man with a beard.

He carries a sword with him.

He marches attentively forward and backwards.

He salutes and bows down when the king and queen are around.

Archard accompanies the lord and his lady on their national tours.

Archard accompanied the lord on his visits to the dockyard, vineyards and farmyards.

Archard was rewarded with an award of bravery and loyalty.

Archard wrote a thank you card to the royal family for their trust and care.

Archard has one weird weakness, he is scared of lizards.

Archard tries to overcome this awkward fear of lizards.

He cannot afford to lose his position over this absurd fear.

Date			
Words per minute			
Number of Errors			

Say the name of each picture and listen to the beginning sound. Circle 'rd' or 'nd'.

rd

rd nd	rd nd	rd nd
rd nd	rd nd	rd nd
rd nd	rd nd	rd nd

Find and circle the words written below.

beard   word   nerd

bird   leopard   herd

rd

w	r	w	o	r	d	s	k
b	r	w	r	h	j	w	l
i	g	i	w	h	d	r	n
r	h	e	n	r	v	e	e
d	w	h	a	k	n	n	r
a	h	e	r	d	l	i	d
d	b	j	x	h	b	e	g
e	l	e	o	p	a	r	d

Write a story using any five words from the word bank.

rd

Beard   heard   word   curd
third   herd   nerd   bird   wizard
Card   custard   yard   hard

Find and circle the words written below.

work   mark   tank

pond   bird   rock

w	k	o	w	g	h	s	r
r	r	w	o	h	j	d	o
m	o	t	r	e	r	o	c
s	h	e	k	t	v	g	k
p	o	n	d	e	n	n	k
a	h	k	r	j	l	i	l
d	m	a	r	k	k	e	e
e	x	k	b	i	r	d	k

Find and circle the words written below.

Drink   word   shock

mend   pork   cord

w	m	e	n	d	h	s	r
r	r	w	o	r	d	d	k
d	o	c	o	r	d	o	c
r	h	e	k	t	v	g	k
i	o	n	d	e	n	n	k
n	h	k	r	j	l	i	l
k	s	h	o	c	k	e	e
e	x	k	p	o	r	k	l

Resource: Cut, Laminate and use it as a resource.

Circle all the 'ck' words.

Lucky Bucky

Bucky is the name of a yellow duck. Bucky has a long neck. Bucky is a lucky duck. Whenever bucky pecks his beak in the water it catches a fish. All the ducks call him "lucky Bucky". Bucky has a friend named Puck. Puck is a white duck. Puck and Bucky spend their day sitting on their favorite rock at the dock. They peck, lick and quack all day long. Bucky likes to sit in the muck. "Yuck Yuck!" says Puck. "Don't sit there." Bucky is quick. He comes out of the muck.

ck

Jack and Nickie

Nickie is packing for her trip. Jack asked Nickie, "What should I pack for the trip?". Nickie said, "Don't forget to pack your socks and favorite clock." Nickie picked all her beautiful frocks with matching necklaces and packed them in the suitcase. Nickie locked the suitcase after checking all her things. "When will we be back from the trip?" asked Jack. Nickie said, "We will be back in a week, don't forget to pack your black shoes and red jacket." Nickie forgot to pack her neck pillow. Jack saw the neck pillow lying beside the checkerboard. Jack gave the neck pillow to his sister.

nk

The Pink trunk

Mom told Josh to clean the junk from his room. She asked him to put all his old toys in the pink trunk. Mom said, "Think wisely and choose all the toys that can be given to charity." Josh was blank for a while. He drank milk and started to think. Josh dunked a chunk of cookie into the milk and ate it. In a blink of an eye, he made up his mind. Josh saw a box under the bunk bed. He found a toy monk and a funny skunk to put inside the pink tank. He also put a piggy bank, an ink pen, soldier's tank and a beautiful plank in the pink trunk.

Circle all the 'nk' words.

nk

Frank goes to the Bank

Frank needed to go to the bank. He ironed the wrinkle shirt and wore it. He checked his car's tank. The tank was filled up with gas. On the way to the bank, Frank saw an old man sitting on a wooden plank. Frank drove by the junkyard and saw a pink vintage car. Frank went blank while watching the pink car. Cars started honking behind Frank's car. "Honk, honk! Start driving man!" Said the man, driving beside Frank's car. Franked winked at the man and said, I am sorry man!" Frank stopped thinking about the pink vintage car and started driving again. Frank saw a punk walking on the road. Frank stopped the car at the traffic signal and saw a monkey siting on the tree trunk. The monkey was eating a chunk of bread and drinking juice. Frank reached the bank and parked the car.

Mask's Task

The teacher gave Jim a task. Jim asked the teacher, "What is the task, Miss? The teacher told Jim, "You have to make an animal mask by dusk tomorrow." Jim walked briskly and went home. Jim took out a box with junk, maybe he could find something he could use for the mask. He found an empty flask, a whisk, a tusk, a disk and some husk. Jim sat down on the desk and started working on the mask. He looked at all the objects he found from the junk box and thought to make an elephant mask using the tusk, disk and husk.

Corn's Husk

Sasha was sitting on the desk, working on her final task. She was drawing an elephant's tusk. She was feeling hungry and was waiting for the bell to ring so that she could eat, but first she would have to remove the corn's husk. But the period was not over yet. The teacher said, "You can ask me if you have any questions. The notes are kept on the desk." Sasha looked at the watch and the bell rang. Sasha jumped up and whisked out of the classroom. Sasha was so hungry that she risked jumping over the fence which was not allowed. Sasha tripped over on a cat which was basking in the sun. She yelled, "Please help!"

rk

Clark the Clerk

Clark works as a clerk at an office. He eats his lunch with his special silver fork. He likes to eat pork. Clark the clerk removes the bottle cork and looks everywhere for a glass. He looks for a glass in the kitchen. The kitchen is dark. Clark turns the light on and finds a glass to pour his drink. Clark smirks and finishes his lunch. Clark goes to the park for a walk. A dog barks at Clark. Clark feeds him the leftover pork. Clark bumps into a stork. "What a dork I am!" Says Clark. "I am sorry, I will mark your spot! Stork." Says, Clark to the Stork.

> Resource: Cut, laminate and use it as a resource.
>
> Circle all the 'rk' words.

Burk's Artwork

Burk lives in Denmark. Burk has a brown birthmark on his left cheek. He is in third grade. He believes in teamwork. Burk always completes his homework on time. Burk is always first in finishing his classwork. No one is as sharp as Burk. Burk's teacher calls him little artist because of his exceptional artwork. His artwork includes a beautiful shark made out of recycled papers and an ark made with toothpicks. Burk also made a park using different cardboard pieces. One of Burk's artworks was a view of a dark night. Burk won a prize at an art competition for making a stork out of cotton and feathers. All the students lurk at Burk's craftwork, whenever he is in the middle of an artwork.

What's that sound in the pond?

Rand likes to sit beside the pond. Rand fantasizes about the nature that surrounds him. He has a round ball. Rand picks up the round ball from the ground. There is a beautiful pond in the sandy ground. Rand looks at all the small creatures in the pond. "Croak" "Croak", Rand hears a strange sound. "What's that sound in the pond?" The frog says, "It's me Rand. Croak, Croak. I'm making this sound. Can you help me send this message to my friend?" Rand says, "Let me help you send this message to your friend." "Quack" "Quack", Rand hears a strange sound coming from the pond. "What's that sound in the pond?" The duck says, "It's me Rand. Quack, Quack! I'm making this sound. Can you give me a hand? I want to come out of this pond." Rand says, "Let me give you a hand, to come out of the pond." "Buzz" "Buzz", Rand hears a strange sound. What's that sound in the pond? The bee says, "It's me Rand. "Buzz" "Buzz". I'm making this sound. Can you help me bend this flower stem? Rand says, "Let me help you bend this flower stem." Rand helped all the animals in the pond.

106

Sandy's Wand

Sandy is a kind girl. She has a magical wand. Sandy is really fond of her golden wand. Sandy goes to the beach. She wants to make the biggest sand castle ever. Sandy waves her wand in the air, wind starts blowing and a big sand castle appears in front of her. While playing in the big sand castle, a paper plane lands in front of Sandy. Sandy pretends to be the pilot of the plane and she plays with the paper plane. Sandy wants the plane to be grand. She looks all around the sand castle for her wand. But she could not find her wand. She sees a group of kids playing in a band. She goes up to the band and asks them, "Have you seen my brand-new golden magical wand?" The kids in the band reply, "We have not seen your brand-new wand. But we can help you find your magical wand". Sandy replies to them, "Thank you! It's very kind of you all."

rd

The Nerd Bird

Once upon a time there lived a bird. His name was Richard. Everyone called him Nerd Richard. Richard the bird was a bookworm. He loved learning new words from the different stories he read. He read a wonderful story about a herd of sheep. The herd of sheep lived in a yard without any shepherd to take care of them. It was hard for the herd to protect themselves. A leopard roamed around the herd. All the sheep united and decided never to be alone. The herd went to the orchard fields and everywhere else as a group. The leopard never got the chance to attack the herd. Richard the bird learned the lesson on unity from the story.

rd

Royal Guard Archard

Archard is a security guard at the castle. He is a handsome man with a beard. He carries a sword with him. He marches attentively forward and backwards. He salutes and bows down when the king and queen are around. Archard accompanies the lord and his lady on their national tours. Archard accompanied the lord on his visits to the dockyard, vineyards and farmyards. Archard was rewarded with an award of bravery and loyalty. Archard wrote a thank you card to the royal family for their trust and care. Archard has one weird weakness, he is scared of lizards. Archard tries to overcome this awkward fear of lizards. He cannot afford to lose his position over this absurd fear.

Made in the USA
Las Vegas, NV
07 September 2023

77177813R00066